MAR 2017

REAL HEROES OF SPORTS
BREAKING BARRIERS

BY HANS HETRICK

CAPSTONE PRESS
a capstone imprint

Sports Illustrated Kids Stats & Stories are published by Capstone Press,
1710 Roe Crest Drive, North Mankato, Minnesota 56003.
www.mycapstone.com

Library of Congress Cataloging-in-Publication Data
Cataloging in Publication info is available at the Library of Congress website.

ISBN 978-1-5157-4434-4 (hardcover)
ISBN 978-1-5157-4446-7 (paperback)
ISBN 978-1-5157-4459-7 (eBook pdf)

Editorial Credits
Nate LeBoutillier, editor; Terri Poburka, designer;
Eric Gohl, media specialist; Gene Bentdahl, production

Photo Credits
Alamy: Outdoor-Archiv, 28–29; AP Photo: 9; Capstone: cover (top left & bottom left);
Courtesy of Steve Guinan and Guy Stout/www.toledotroopers.com: 14, 15, 16, 17;
Getty Images: Bettmann, 11 (right), Focus On Sport, 18, Michael Rougier, 27, Rich
Clarkson, 10–11, Sports Studio Photos, 8, Staff, 26; Newscom: ZUMA Press/Junior
Lago, 20, ZUMA Press/Rodolfo Buhrer, 13; Shutterstock: Ksanawo, cover (bottom
right), 1, Snap2Art, cover (top right); Sports Illustrated: John G. Zimmerman, 22, 23,
Mark Kauffman, 5, 6–7 (all), 25 (top), Robert Beck, 21, Tony Triolo, 12, 25 (bottom)

Design Elements: Shutterstock

Printed in the United States of America.
010054S17

Table of
CONTENTS

DREAMS AND DETERMINATION

There are a few athletes that possess an unmatched drive. They defy pressure, pain, and setback. They chase their dreams even when most people tell them to stop. Some of these remarkable athletes become heroes.

The athletes in *Breaking Barriers* are real heroes of sports because they pushed the limits of their sport into new territory. They showed the world that athletic excellence can come from anyone, regardless of their background. They overcame challenges that others didn't face. They developed new techniques that took their sport to new heights. By breaking down barriers, these athletes have shown that the limits of our lives can be exceeded by our dreams and our determination.

Jackie
ROBINSON:

Grace Under Fire

Jackie Robinson gained fame for breaking the color barrier in sports. This fame was well-deserved considering the things Robinson had to endure. Pitchers threw at his head. Baserunners slid at him with their metal spikes aimed at his shins. Catchers spit on his shoes. Throughout it all, Robinson kept his cool. By enduring the hatred hurled at him on the baseball diamond and not resorting to violence, the hatred appeared all the more unjust.

Jackie Robinson was primarily a second baseman for the Dodgers but also played first and third base.

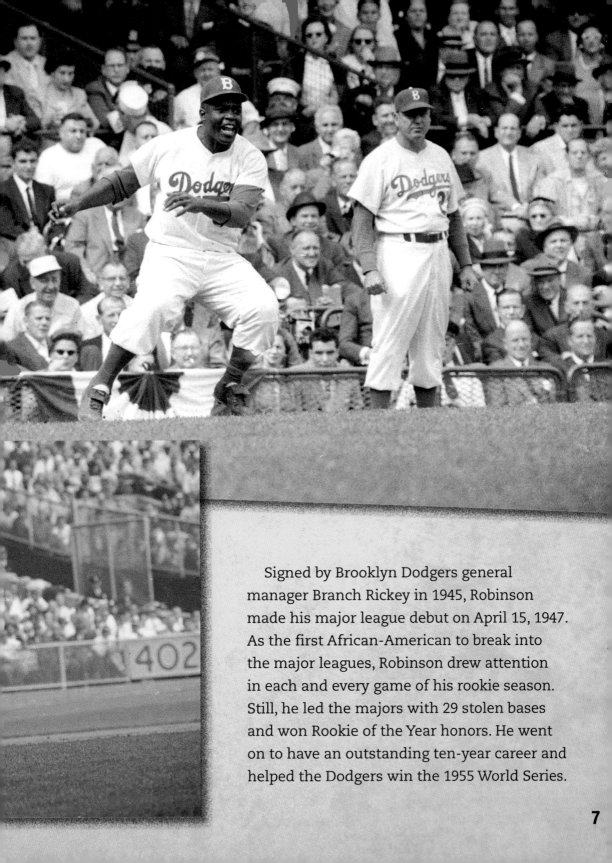

Signed by Brooklyn Dodgers general
manager Branch Rickey in 1945, Robinson
made his major league debut on April 15, 1947.
As the first African-American to break into
the major leagues, Robinson drew attention
in each and every game of his rookie season.
Still, he led the majors with 29 stolen bases
and won Rookie of the Year honors. He went
on to have an outstanding ten-year career and
helped the Dodgers win the 1955 World Series.

ON THE CUTTING EDGE

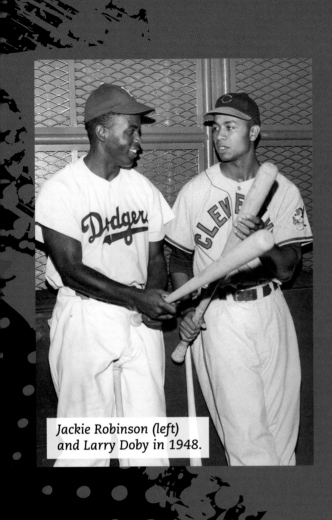

Jackie Robinson (left) and Larry Doby in 1948.

Larry Doby was the second African-American player to play major league baseball. He joined the Cleveland Indians in 1948, a year after Jackie Robinson's debut. He also became the second African-American to manage a team. He was, however, the first African-American to win a World Series when Cleveland won it all in 1948.

After he retired from baseball, Robinson put all of his energy into breaking down barriers for African-Americans. He promoted the advancement of African-Americans in the business world. In 1957 Robinson was hired as an executive at Chock full o'Nuts coffee company, becoming the first African-American vice president of a major American corporation. He helped found the black-owned Freedom National Bank in Harlem. The bank provided loans to African-Americans because white-owned banks often denied loan requests from black applicants. He also started the Jackie Robinson Construction Company, which built housing for low-income families.

Jackie Robinson (foreground) participates in a civil rights march in Frankfurt, Kentucky, in 1964.

Robinson was also a major participant in the civil rights movement. He marched with Martin Luther King Jr. He delivered stirring speeches at rallies. He used his celebrity to raise money for the movement. Robinson woke up every day and did everything he could to improve the lives of African-Americans. He once said, "A life is not important except in the impact it has on other lives." Jackie Robinson never stopped fighting to break down the barriers that locked millions of African-Americans in poverty and inequality.

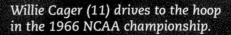
Willie Cager (11) drives to the hoop in the 1966 NCAA championship.

Texas
WESTERN:

The Upset of Inequality

The Texas Western Miners were colossal underdogs in the 1966 NCAA men's basketball championship. The Miners came from a small school with a young coach, Don Haskins. Haskins' 1966 team looked different from most NCAA teams. The 1966 Miners consisted of seven African-Americans, four Caucasians, and one Latino. Earlier in the season, the Miners had become the first college team to start five African-Americans.

The Miners finished the 1965–66 regular season with a sparkling 23–1 record, though they played smaller schools. In the NCAA tournament, Texas Western won thrilling games in overtime in the second and third rounds, including a monumental double overtime over heavily-favored Kansas.

Heroic FACT

Kentucky finally began to recruit black players by 1969. Today, more players from Kentucky than any other school have joined the National Basketball Association.

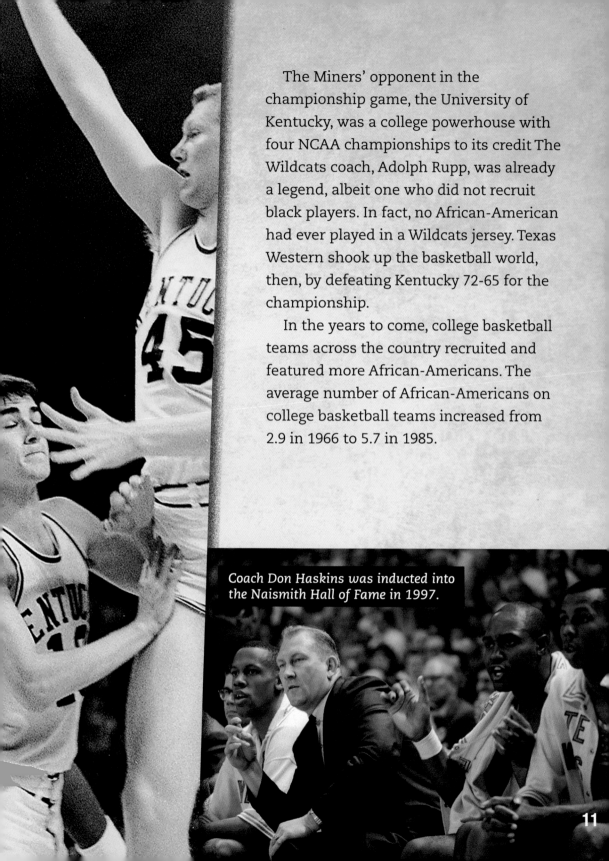

The Miners' opponent in the championship game, the University of Kentucky, was a college powerhouse with four NCAA championships to its credit The Wildcats coach, Adolph Rupp, was already a legend, albeit one who did not recruit black players. In fact, no African-American had ever played in a Wildcats jersey. Texas Western shook up the basketball world, then, by defeating Kentucky 72-65 for the championship.

In the years to come, college basketball teams across the country recruited and featured more African-Americans. The average number of African-Americans on college basketball teams increased from 2.9 in 1966 to 5.7 in 1985.

Coach Don Haskins was inducted into the Naismith Hall of Fame in 1997.

Nadia
COMANECI:
Perfection Personified

Romanian gymnast Nadia Comaneci was perfect at the 1976 Olympics. In fact, she was perfect seven times. Comaneci scored the first perfect ten score in the history of Olympic gymnastics. After her first flawless routine on the compulsory uneven bars, the scoreboard showed a score of 1.00. The scoreboard wasn't big enough to display 10.00. The Montreal crowd was confused at first. When they realized they had just witnessed perfection, fans roared in approval.

Nadia Comaneci

Comaneci won three gold medals, one silver, and one bronze at the 1976 Olympics. And at 14 years old, she became the youngest gymnast to win the individual all-around Olympic gold medal.

Comaneci became the darling of the Olympics. She mesmerized the world with her incredible skill and precision. She charmed the world with her grace and exquisite movements. Comaneci combined acrobatic excellence and beautiful dance. That's how she became known as "Little Miss Perfect".

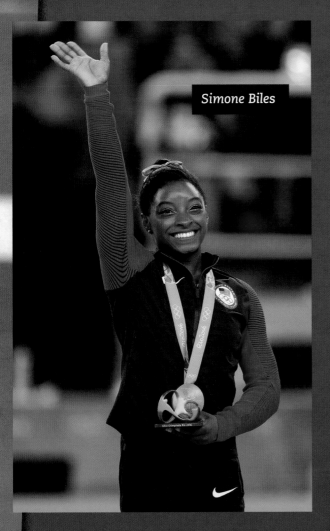

Simone Biles

GOLDEN GIRL

Going into the 2016 Olympics in Rio de Janeiro, American gymnast Simone Biles seemed destined for golden results. After all, the 19-year-old had claimed three all-around world championships leading up to the Rio Games. Biles did not disappoint. The speedy and powerful U.S. gymnast captured five medals at the 2016 Olympics, including the all-around gold.

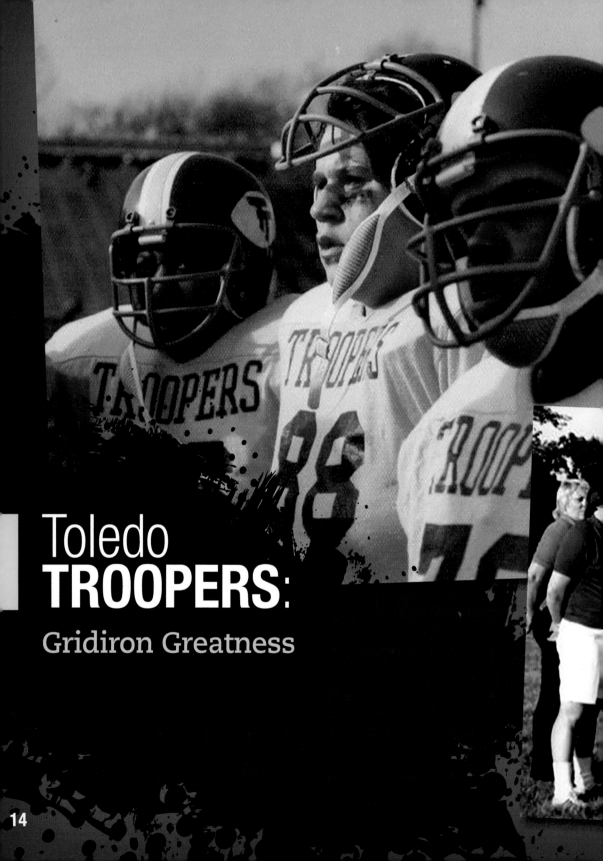

Toledo
TROOPERS:

Gridiron Greatness

The Toledo Troopers were a group of women who loved to play football—hard-hitting football. And they were good. The roster of the Troopers, from Toledo, Ohio, featured factory workers, beauticians, homemakers, businesswomen, and mothers. For five months each year, the Troopers' coach, Bill Stout, worked his players into the ground during grueling, five-hour practices. The grueling practices paid off. The Troopers won Women's Pro Football League championships in 1971, 1972, and 1973.

Heroic FACT

Though the Toledo Troopers no longer exist, a new women's team called the Toledo Reign still plays pro football in Toledo, Ohio.

Toledo Troopers team photo

Due to the adoption of a new federal rule in 1972 calling for equality in athletics, women's sports were gaining steam in the early 1970s. In 1974 the National Women's Football League (NWFL) was formed. Along with the Troopers, the league included the California Mustangs, Columbus Pacesetters, Dallas Bluebonnets, Detroit Demons, Fort Worth Shamrocks, and Los Angeles Dandelions. Two more teams, the Oklahoma City Dolls

and Tucson Wild Kittens, joined in 1976. The Toledo Troopers won the championship each year from 1974 to 1977.

The NWFL shut down in 1979 due to financial struggles. The Troopers ended their run with 64 wins and only 4 losses. The Pro Football Hall of Fame recognized the Toledo Troopers as the professional football team with the highest winning percentage in the history of the sport.

TOP TROOPER

Linda Jefferson, the star running back of the Toledo Troopers, gained 8,207 yards and scored 140 touchdowns in her career. After her football-playing days, Jefferson spent 35 years as a teacher assistant specializing in work with autistic children. She was inducted into the Semi-Pro Football Hall of Fame in 2002.

Linda Jefferson

Roberto CLEMENTE:

A Saint in Cleats

Heroic FACT

The final hit of Roberto Clemente's career was his 3,000th. In 18 years of Major League Baseball, Clemente played 2,459 games, won four batting titles, and helped Pittsburgh capture World Series titles in 1960 and 1971.

On the field, Roberto Clemente was revered for his baseball excellence. Off the field, he inspired legions of people through his charity, strong work ethic, and Puerto Rican pride.

After breaking into the majors in 1955, Clemente became one of the best rightfielders to ever play the game. The Pittsburgh Pirate had a rocket launcher for a right arm and a sticky glove. As a hitter, he was consistently at the top of the league in batting average and extra base hits. He won 12 straight Gold Gloves and four National League batting titles. Clemente became the first Latino to win both the National League MVP (in 1966) and the World Series MVP (in 1971).

Off the field, Clemente used his time and money to help others. He held baseball clinics for children from low-income families and traveled the Americas providing aid to those in need. Tragically, Clemente was killed at age 38 in a plane crash in 1972. He was flying from his native Puerto Rico to Nicaragua in a plane loaded with supplies for the victims of an earthquake. Three months later, Clemente became the first Latino inducted into the Baseball Hall of Fame.

Roberto Clemente remains one of Puerto Rico's greatest heroes. Clemente inspired a new generation of baseball players from the Caribbean nations. He also set a example of generosity and compassion for all people through his baseball excellence, his charity, and his pride.

Michael
PHELPS:

King of the Pool

There are normal, everyday people, and then there are Olympians. There are normal, everyday Olympians, and then there's Michael Phelps. After another brilliant Olympic run in 2016 in Rio de Janeiro, the U.S. swimmer stood far and away as the most decorated and dominant athlete in modern Olympic history.

Phelps' first Olympic experience began in 2000 in Sydney, Australia, at the tender age of 15. Young Phelps swam his way to a fifth-place finish in the 200-meter butterfly. The next year, Phelps set his first world record in a different event—the 400-meter freestyle. By the time the next Olympics rolled around, Phelps was ready for glory. In the 2004 Games in Athens, Greece, Phelps captured six gold medals and

two bronze medals. In the 2008 Games in Beijing, China, Phelps was a force of nature, winning gold in all eight of his events and setting seven world records. He added seven medals (five gold) in London in 2012 and six more in Rio in 2016.

In the end, Phelps broke through the barrier of what was previously considered Olympic excellence. His achievements seem insurmountable.

Heroic FACT

After his final race at the 2016 Olympics, Michael Phelps had garnered 23 Olympic gold medals and 28 medals overall. The next closest Olympian in gold medals is Jamaican sprinter Usain Bolt with nine.

Althea
GIBSON:
Tennis
Trailblazer

Althea Gibson traveled a long road from an eighth-grade dropout to shaking hands with the queen of England. Gibson was raised on 143rd Street in Harlem, New York. During the day, the city blocked off 143rd Street, so the neighborhood children could play organized sports. Gibson's earliest favorites included basketball and paddle tennis. She became the New York City women's paddle tennis champion at age 12. From there she naturally gravitated toward tennis.

As a teen, Gibson began playing—and winning—tournaments that were sponsored by the American Tennis Association (ATA), an all-black association. Gibson's raw talent caught the attention of Dr. Hubert Eaton and Dr. Walter Johnson, two high-profile ATA members. The doctors also soon learned that Gibson couldn't stand going to school and often skipped classes. The doctors took Gibson under their wings and she blossomed. She returned to school and graduated, and then she got a degree at Florida A&M University at age 25.

Alice Marble, a former world number one tennis player, urged the U.S. Lawn Tennis Association to invite Gibson to the U.S. Nationals. In 1950 Gibson became the first African-American woman to play in the U.S. Nationals. She lost a close match to Louise Brough, winner of the last three Wimbledon championships, in the second round.

The world tennis circuit was a lonely road for Gibson. She was the only player of color at most tournaments, and, as a result, many players ignored her. But

Gibson kept playing and improving until she hit her prime in 1956. That year, she became the first black woman to win the French Open. In 1957 she became the first African-American woman to win the U.S. Nationals and Wimbledon, where she shook hands with England's Queen Elizabeth II. Gibson was named Female Athlete of the Year by the *Associated Press* in 1957 and 1958. She then became just the second African-American to receive a ticker tape parade in New York City.

DOUBLY IMPRESSIVE

Angela Buxton was a Jewish tennis player from England. Althea Gibson was an black tennis player from America. Both experienced their share of prejudice. When they found each other, they became an unstoppable doubles team. They won the doubles title at the 1956 French Open. Unfortunately, their partnership was short-lived. Buxton suffered a career-ending injury soon after their title.

Roger
BANNISTER:
Running Doctor

In the early 1950s, two seemingly mystical barriers were yet to be broken: climbing Mt. Everest and running a mile in four minutes or less. Edmund Hillary and Tenzing Norgay summited Mt. Everest in 1953. Roger Bannister broke the four-minute mile the very next year.

Roger Bannister was not only a gifted runner, he was a curious medical student at Oxford University. Bannister used his medical know-how to study the demands of running. He discovered that running at a set pace required less oxygen than a varied pace did. Based on his discovery, Bannister concentrated on his quarter-mile splits in training. In five months, he reduced his quarter-mile times from 63 seconds to 59 seconds.

Bannister broke the four-minute barrier in Oxford, England, on May 6, 1954, in a steady rain and high winds. After he crossed the finish line with a time of 3 minutes, 59.4 seconds, Bannister collapsed into the arms of a friend. Today, more people have climbed Mt. Everest than have run a mile under four minutes.

Roger Bannister (329) runs at the 1954 British Empire and Commonwealth Games.

Heroic FACT

In the 1970s, Roger Bannister became the chairman of Britain's Sports Council. He promoted running as a part of good health practices.

Roger Bannister (second from left) runs with his children (from left to right), Charlotte, Thurstan, Erin, and Clive, in 1974.

Dick
FOSBURY:
Father of the Flop

In 1963 Dick Fosbury was a tall and awkward teenager from Medford, Oregon, who just wanted to make the high school track and field team. He figured the high jump was his best chance. At the time, high jumpers cleared the bar using one of two methods. The first, called the "Scissors," involved flinging one leg and then the other over the bar and landing on one's feet. High jumpers using the "Western Roll" cleared the bar face first, then rolled their legs over. Fosbury couldn't clear the minimum 5-foot-4 height with either technique, so he created a new one by jumping with his back to the bar.

With practice Fosbury improved quickly. Through careful study, he perfected his new method. At the 1968 Olympics, Fosbury shocked the world, winning the Olympic gold medal with an impressive jump of 7-foot-4.25 (2.24 meters). What's more, all high jumpers today use "The Fosbury Flop."

Heroic FACT

Dick Fosbury was elected to the U.S. Track and Field Hall of Fame in 1993. That was the same year the high jump record—which still stands today—was set by Javier Sotomayor of Cuba with a jump of 8 feet and a quarter inch (2.45 m).

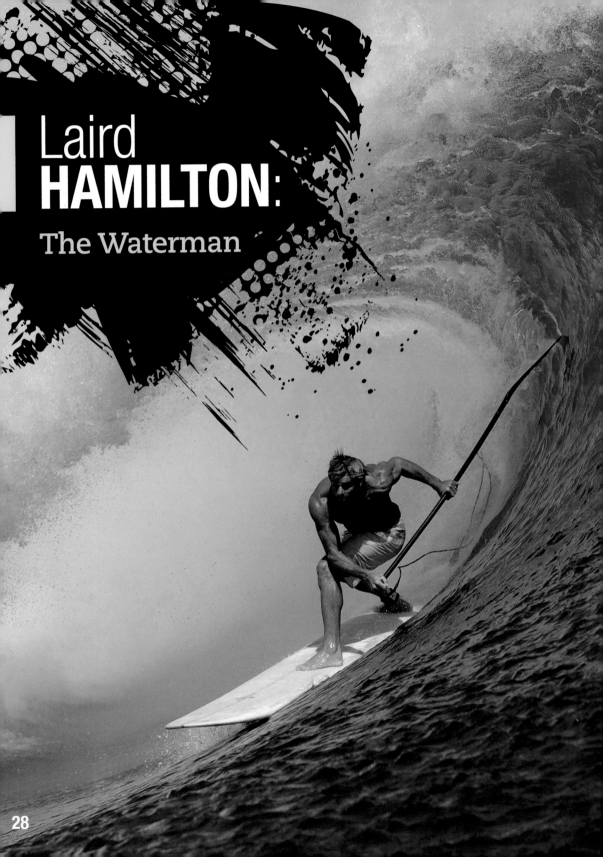

Laird
HAMILTON:
The Waterman

Surfers are on an endless quest to find the ultimate wave. No surfer has pursued the ultimate wave with as much passion as Laird Hamilton. Hamilton pushed the boundaries of big wave surfing to their maximum.

Hamilton and his friend Darrick Doerner revolutionized surfing in 1992. They started towing one another into big waves using inflatable boats and Jet Skis. The technique became known as tow-in surfing. Tow-in surfing allowed Hamilton and his friends to ride 80-foot monster waves that were impossible to surf before.

Hamilton cemented his status as a surfing legend on August 17, 2000. He dropped into a huge wave on Tahiti's extremely dangerous Teahupo'o break. When surfers talk about "The Wave," they're talking about Hamilton's ride that morning.

"You wait your whole life for a moment," Hamilton said. "And I will prepare for 50 years to have one ride." For all his innovations and death-defying feats, many surfers worldwide call him "The Waterman."

Heroic FACT

Garret McNamara broke the world record for surfing the biggest wave on January 28, 2013. McNamara caught a tremendous wave estimated at around 100 feet tall off the coast of Nazare, Portugal.

Glossary

Caucasian – person who is of white European descent and not of Hispanic origin

charity – a kindness shown by helping someone in need

circuit – a series of contests that leads to a single championship

equality – the state of being equal, especially in terms of opportunity, status, and rights

gravitate – move toward or be attracted to a person, place, or thing

innovation – the creation of new ideas, devices, or methods

plateau – an area of high, flat land

powerhouse – a person or thing of great energy, strength, or power

prejudice – an opinion about others that is unfair or not based on facts

recruit – to ask someone to join a college team

Read More

Buckly, James, Jr. *Who was Roberto Clemente?* New York: Grosset and Dunlap, 2014.

Omoth, Tyler. *Six Degrees of David Ortiz: Connecting Baseball Stars*. Six Degrees of Sports. N. Mankato, Minn.: Capstone, 2015.

Tougas, Joe. *Real Heroes of Sports: Heroic Comebacks*. Real Heroes of Sports. N. Mankato, Minn.: Capstone, 2017.

Internet Links

FactHound offers a safe, fun way to find Internet sites related to this book. All of the sites on FactHound have been researched by our staff.

Here's all you do:

Visit *www.facthound.com*

Type in this code: 9781515744344

Check out projects, games and lots more at **www.capstonekids.com**

Index